RELICS OF THE SAINTS

January – February

Richard G. Cannuli, O.S.A.

Marcelle Bartolo-Abela

First published in 2015 by
HOPE AND LIFE PRESS

Relics of the Saints: January – February

Volume #1 in the Hope and Life Press series on RELICS OF THE SAINTS.

ISBN 978-0-692-59615-9

Copyright © 2015 Richard G. Cannuli, O.S.A., and Marcelle Bartolo-Abela – All rights reserved.

Front cover shows the left foremost icon from the *Story of the Holy Girdle* by the hand of Bernando Daddi (1337-38), found above the high altar in the Duomo di Prato, Italy.

Published by
HOPE AND LIFE PRESS
2312 Chemin Herron #A, Dorval QC, H9S 1C5 Canada; and
P.O. Box 37, East Longmeadow, MA 01028, USA.
http://hopeandlifepress.com
hopeandlifepress@gmail.com

All rights reserved. No part of this work may be reproduced, stored in a retrieval system, or submitted in any form or by any means, electronic, mechanical, photocopying, recording or otherwise, without the prior written permission of the publisher. This book may not be lent, resold, hired out or otherwise disposed of by way of trade in any form of binding or cover other than that in which it is published, without the prior written consent of the published.

Printed in the United States of America.

CONTENTS

RELICS OF THE SAINTS – JANUARY

1. The Blessed Virgin Mary — 7
2. Saint Agnes of Rome — 14
3. Saint André Bessette — 15
4. Blessed Angelo Paoli — 16
5. Saint Anthony the Great — 17
6. Saint Basil of Caesarea — 18
7. Saint Elizabeth Ann Seton — 19
8. Saint Ephraim the Syrian — 20
9. Saint Fulgentius of Ruspe — 21
10. Saint Genevieve of Paris — 22
11. Saint Gregory of Nazianzus — 23
12. Saint Hilary of Poitiers — 24
13. Saint John the Baptist — 25
14. Saint John Bosco — 26
15. Saint John Chrysostom — 27
16. Saint John Nepomucene Neumann — 28
17. Saint Marcella of Rome — 29
18. Saint Maximus the Hagiorite — 30
19. Saint Rafaela Maria Porras — 31
20. Saint Romuald — 32
21. Saint Sebastian — 33
22. Saint Seraphim of Sarov — 34
23. Saint Thomas Aquinas — 35
24. The Three Kings — 36

RELICS OF THE SAINTS – FEBRUARY

25. Saint Agatha — 39
26. Blessed Angelo of Furci — 40
27. Blessed Anselm Polanco Fontecha — 41
28. Saint Blaise — 42
29. Saint Claude de la Colombière — 43
30. Saint Cyril and Saint Methodius — 44
31. Saint Cyril of Jerusalem — 45
32. Saint Gabriel of the Addolorata and Saint Paul of the Cross — 46
33. The Japanese Martyrs — 48

34. Saint Josephine Bakhita	49
35. Saint Miguel Febres Cordero Muñoz	50
36. Saint Perpetua and Saint Felicity	51
37. Blessed Pius IX	52
38. Saint Polycarp	53
39. Saint Symeon the God-Receiver	54
40. Blessed Simon Fidati	55
41. Blessed Stefano Bellesini	56
42. Saint Valentine	57
References	59
About the Authors	63
Hope and Life Press Books	65

RELICS OF THE SAINTS

JANUARY

BLESSED VIRGIN MARY
MOTHER OF GOD AND QUEEN OF HEAVEN

Ex velo Beata Mariae Virgine (center)

Small threads from the silk veil of the Blessed Virgin Mary, surrounded by relics of Saint Joseph, Saint Anne, Saint Charles Borromeo, Saint Vincent de Paule, and Saint Vincent Ferrer. Second class relic in large Baroque, gilt bronze, framed multi-reliquary, hand carved and handmade in the 1700s.

The Blessed Virgin Mary (Maryam of Nazareth, n. d.) is the Mother of Our Lord, Jesus Christ, the only-begotten Son of God (*Theotokos*; First Council of Ephesus, 431). She was assumed body and soul into heaven, and is the Queen of heaven and earth (Pope Pius XII, 1950, 1954). The Virgin Mary is the Woman described in the books of Genesis (3:15), the Psalms (45:9), and Revelation (12:1-5). She is the Immaculate Conception (Pope Pius IX, 1854) and the Ever-Virgin (Second Council of Constantinople, 553).

Detail of the threads from the veil

A small piece of the Virgin's veil, that she was reportedly wearing when giving birth to Jesus Christ, was originally in the possession of the Emperor Charlemagne who received it as a gift from the Byzantine Empress Irene of Constantinople. It was gifted by Charlemagne's grandson, Charles II, to the Cathédrale Notre-Dame de Chartres, Chartres, France in 876. Other portions of the veil can be found in churches across Italy, in Cologne and Mainz, Germany; and in Prague, Czech Republic among others.

Ex Domus Lauretana

Small stone from one of the walls in the Holy House of the Blessed Virgin Mary that can be found in Loreto, Italy. The Holy House is where the Virgin was born, and the Annunciation by the Angel Gabriel and the Incarnation occurred (Lk 1:26-38). The Holy House was transported through many routes from its original place in Nazareth, Israel to Loreto, Ancona, Italy, where it is now housed at the Basilica Della Santa Casa. Second class relic.

Ex velo Lauretana

Large portion of the original black veil that covered the statue of the Madonna di Loreto, both destroyed in a fire in 1921. Considered a second class relic, translation overleaf.

Declaration

"I, the undersigned custodian of the Holy House of Loreto, attest that the black veil that is sealed and affixed to this note, covered the Holy Statue of Our Lady of Loreto on Maundy Thursday and Good Friday, and was then touched to the Holy Walls and the Holy Bowl of the Blessed Virgin, which is conserved in this her Holy House. In faith, Loreto, from the Custodian this 31st August, 1845. (Signed)."

Ex fascia Beata Virgine Mariae

Large piece from the girdle of the Blessed Virgin Mary, which she gave to the Apostle Thomas upon her Assumption. Large portions of the girdle can be found at Vatopedi Monastery, Mount Athos, Greece; at the Monastery of Trier, Germany; and in Georgia. Second class relic.

Ex capillis, ex velo, ex veste, ex sepulchro Beata Virgine Mariae

Short strand of hair, small pieces of the silk veil and colored robe, and a stone from the tomb of the Blessed Virgin Mary. The Virgin's locks of hair, robe, and veil were originally kept by the Patriarchs of Jerusalem, until the Patriarch Saint Juvenal gave them to the Empress Saint Pulcheria, who gifted them to the city of Constantinople. The Virgin's hair can now be found in the great reliquary at the Duomo di Messina, Sicily. The Virgin's tomb can be found in the crypt of the Church of the Assumption, Kidron Valley (valley of Josaphat), Jerusalem, Israel. First, second, and third class relics.

Detail of the strand of hair (left) and small piece of the silk veil (right)

Detail of the small piece of the vestment (left) and stone from the tomb (right)

SAINT AGNES OF ROME

Saint Agnes of Rome (c. 291 – c. 304) was born to a noble Roman family. She was martyred at 12 years of age for being Christian (Schaff, 2009) after having steadfastly refused to give up her virginity to some young Roman men who had felt slighted by her refusal. Saint Agnes was buried near Via Nomentana, Rome, Italy.

Ex ossibus Sancta Agnetis

Small piece of bone of Saint Agnes, Virgin and Martyr. Many of her bones can be found underneath the main altar in the Chiesa di Sant'Agnese Fuori le Mura, Rome, Italy, which was built above her tomb. The skull of Saint Agnes can be found at the Chiesa di Sant'Agnese in Agone, Piazza Navona, also in Rome. First class relic.

SAINT ANDRÉ BESSETTE

Saint André Bessette (Brother André; 1845 – 1937) was a Canadian orphan who became a sickly, lay brother with the Congregation of the Holy Cross (2014), serving as doorman and janitor. He had little-to-no formal education. Saint André became the first male saint of Quebec, credited with thousands of spontaneous healings through prayer and touch from his great devotion to Saint Joseph, earning the title of "Miracle Man of Montreal." Saint André was the founder and builder of L'Oratoire Saint-Joseph du Mont-Royal.

Ex sanguine Saint André Bessette

Small piece of linen with the blood of Saint André Bessette. His remains can be found in the tomb beneath the main chapel in the Minor Basilica of Saint Joseph's Oratory in Montreal, Quebec, Canada. First and second class relics.

BLESSED ANGELO PAOLI

Blessed Angelo Paoli (1642 – 1720) was an Italian priest with the Calced Carmelites, who served as master of novices, bursar, organist, and sacristan. People regarded him as the "father of the poor [and] Father Charity" because of his notable compassion and charity towards the sick poor in the public hospitals of Rome, Italy (Herbermann, 1913). Blessed Angelo regarded Divine Providence as "a pantry where nothing is ever wanting" (The British Province of Carmelites, 2013).

Ex ossibus Beatus Angeli Paoli

Substantial piece of bone of Blessed Angelo Paoli. His body can be found in the left nave of the Basilica Minore di Santi Silvestro e Martino ai Monti, Rome, Italy. First class relic.

SAINT ANTHONY THE GREAT

Saint Anthony the Great (the Abbot, Anthony of the Desert, c. 251 – 356) was an ascetic from Lower Egypt, known as the "Father of All Monks" among the Desert Fathers (Copt-Net Repository, n. d.). He is considered the father of the monastic family (Walsh, 1991). Saint Anthony lived in the Nitrian Desert west of Alexandria, on Pispir Mountain by the Nile, and in the Eastern Desert. He was regularly sought out for words of enlightenment, some of which can be found in *Sayings of the Desert Fathers*.

Ex ossibus Sancte Antonii

Small piece of bone of Saint Anthony the Great. His remains were translated in 361 from the mountain-top cave where he lived to Alexandria, then to Constantinople. The Byzantine Emperor gave them to Count Jocelin, who gifted them to the Church of Saint-Antoine-l'Abbaye, Isère Department, France. First class relic.

SAINT BASIL OF CAESAREA

Saint Basil of Caesarea (the Great; c. 330 – 379) is a Doctor of the Church, one of the Three Holy Hierarchs, and one of the Cappadocian Fathers (McSorley, 1907). He was the Greek bishop of Caesarea Mazaca in Asia Minor, known for his care of the poor; a famous preacher, and theologian who supported the Nicene Creed and fought against Arianism. One of his major written works was *De Spiritu Sancto*. Saint Basil was the father of communal monasticism in Eastern Christianity.

Ex ossibus Sancte Basilii

Bone fragments of Saint Basil of Caesarea, Bishop and Doctor of the Church. His skull can be found at the Monastery of Great Lavra, Mount Athos, Greece. Some of his bones can be found at the Basilica of the Holy Blood, Bruges, Belgium. First class relic.

SAINT ELIZABETH ANN SETON

Saint Elizabeth Ann Seton (1774 – 1821) was the first native-born citizen of the United States of America (USA) to become a saint (Emmitsburg Area Historical Society, 1996). A married, New York socialite and convert from Anglicanism, with great interest in values-based education, she founded the Sisters of Charity of Saint Joseph – the first American congregation of religious sisters – and established the first free Catholic school for girls in the nation. Saint Elizabeth Ann was a prolific writer.

Ex ossibus Saint Elizabeth Ann Seton

Small piece of bone of Saint Elizabeth Ann Seton. Her remains are entombed in the Altar of Relics at the Basilica of the National Shrine of Saint Elizabeth Ann Seton, Emmitsburg, Maryland, US. First class relic.

SAINT EPHRAIM THE SYRIAN

Saint Ephraim the Syrian (c. 306 – 373) is a Doctor of the Church. He was an ascetic deacon, hymnographer, theologian, and confessor (Orthodox Church in America, 1996; Schaff, 2013). His major works include lyric teaching hymns in syllabic verse, the most famous being *Hymns Against Heresies*; together with several inspirational sermons for which he became known as the "Harp of the Spirit." Saint Ephraim also wrote prose biblical exegesis and practical theology for the troubled Church.

Ex ossibus Saint Ephraim

Small piece of bone of Saint Ephraim the Syrian, Doctor and Confessor. His relics can be found at Deir el-Syriani, Wadi El Natrun, Beheira Governorate, Egypt. First class relic.

SAINT FULGENTIUS OF RUSPE

Saint Fulgentius of Ruspe (c. 467 – c. 533) was bishop of Ruspe, Tunisia and an extraordinary preacher. The best theologian of his time, Saint Fulgentius wrote heatedly and skillfully against Arianism and Semi-Pelagianism (Burns, 1995), as well as about the doctrines of grace and predestination of Saint Augustine (Rotelle, 2000). For the latter activity, he earned the title of "Augustine in short [or] the pocket Augustine." Saint Fulgentius was a firm believer in the *filioque* (*Letter to Peter on the Faith* II, 54).

Ex ossibus Sancte Fulgentii

Small piece of bone of Saint Fulgentius of Ruspe, Bishop. Some of his remains were translated to Bourges, France in 714. First class relic.

SAINT GENEVIEVE OF PARIS

Saint Genevieve of Paris (c. 422 – c. 512) was a consecrated virgin and mystic. In 451, she led a prayer marathon with fasting that saved the city of Paris, France from Attila the Hun, by diverting his army and himself away from the city to Orleans (McNamara, Halborg, & Whatley, 1992). Saint Genevieve also acted as intermediary between the people and Childeric I when the latter conquered Paris, persuading him to release all the prisoners.

Ex ossibus Saint Genevieve

Small piece of bone of Saint Genevieve of Paris, Virgin. Some small relics of the saint can be found in her tomb at the Church of Saint-Etienne du Mont, Paris, France. The majority of her remains had been publicly burned during the French Revolution. First class relic.

SAINT GREGORY OF NAZIANZUS

Saint Gregory of Nazianzus (the Theologian; c. 329 – 390) is a Doctor of the Church, one of the Three Holy Hierarchs, and one of the Cappadocian Fathers (Holy Apostles Convent, 2001). He was archbishop of Constantinople and the most accomplished rhetorical stylist in Patristics (McGuckin, 2001). Saint Gregory was considered the "Trinitarian theologian" for his steadfast defense of the doctrine of the Holy Trinity and the single nature of the Godhead. He set forth the idea of the *procession* of the Holy Spirit and established Byzantine theology by introducing Hellenism into the Early Church.

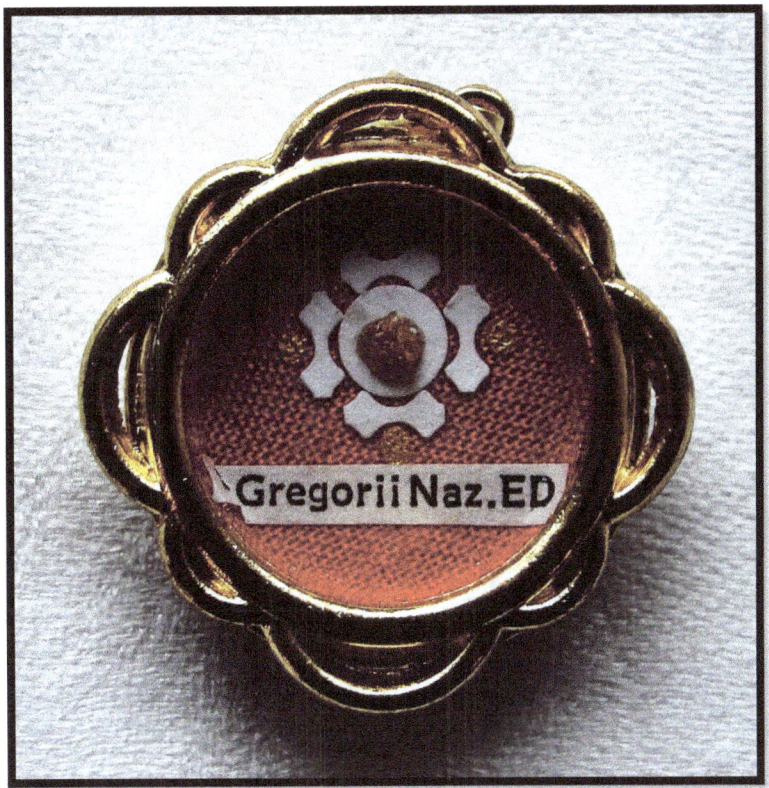

Ex ossibus Sancte Gregorii

Substantial piece of bone of Saint Gregory of Nazianzus, Doctor and Bishop. His relics were translated from Nazianzus to Constantinople in 1204 by the Crusaders, ending up in Rome, Italy. In 2004, many of the saint's relics were returned by Saint John Paul II to the Patriarchal Cathedral of Saint George, Istanbul, Turkey. Some of the relics remained at the Vatican. First class relic.

SAINT HILARY OF POITIERS

Saint Hilary of Poitiers (c. 310 – c. 367) is a Doctor of the Church. Originally married, with a classical education, Saint Hilary abandoned Neo-Platonism for Christianity and eventually became bishop of Poitiers, France by popular vote (Schaff, 2012). He steadfastly fought Arianism in many ways, excommunicating and impeaching various members of the hierarchy, and earning the title "Hammer of the Arians [and] Athanasius of the West." Among Saint Hilary's major works are *De fide Orientalium*, *De synodis*, and *De Trinitate*.

Ex indumentis Saint Hilary

Small piece from the vestment of Saint Hilary of Poitiers, Doctor and Bishop. Some of his relics can be found at the Cathédrale Notre-Dame-du-Puy, Le Puy-en-Velay, France and at L'Église Saint-Hilaire-le-Grand, Poitiers, also in France. Second class relic.

SAINT JOHN THE BAPTIST

Saint John the Baptist (the holy Forerunner, n. d.) is the third cousin of Our Lord, Jesus Christ (Lk 1:5-25); the ascetic prophet with the priesthood of Aaron, and the preacher who publicly denounced the Pharisees and the Sadducees as "offspring of vipers" (Lk 3:7). He baptized Christ in the Jordan River (Mt 3:13-17) and witnessed the Theophany of the Holy Trinity (Orthodox Church in America, 1996). Saint John was beheaded by order of Herod the Tetrarch at the request of his stepdaughter, Salome, and his (brother's) wife, Herodias (Mk 6:14-29), just before the Passover of Christ's public ministry.

Ex ossibus Sancte Joannis

Substantial piece of bone from the skull of Saint John the Baptist, Preacher and Martyr. After being translated from his burial place in Sebastia, Nablus to Valletta, Malta among other places, the saint's skull can now be found at the Chiesa di San Silvestro in Campo Marzio, Rome, Italy. The saint's right hand, by which he had baptized Jesus Christ, can be found at the Grand Church of the Winter Palace, Saint Petersburg, Russia. First class relic.

SAINT JOHN BOSCO

Saint John Bosco (Confessor and Founder; 1815 – 1888) was an Italian Catholic priest, educator, and writer who spent his life helping the poor, street children, and juvenile delinquents, for which he was given the title "Father and Teacher of Youth" (Matz, 2000). He developed the Salesian Preventive System, which consisted of a pedagogy of love rather than punishment (Morrison, 1999). Saint John founded the Institute of the Daughters of Mary, Help of Christians; the Association of Salesian Cooperators, and the *Salesian Bulletin*.

Ex indumentis Sancte Joannis

Small piece from the clothing of Saint John Bosco, Confessor and Founder. His relics can be found at the Basilica di Santa Maria Ausiliatrice, Torino, Italy. Second class relic.

SAINT JOHN CHRYSOSTOM

Saint John Chrysostom (c. 349 – 407) is a Doctor of the Church and one of the Three Holy Hierarchs (Holy Apostles Convent, 2001). As archbishop of Constantinople, he was known for his preaching and zealous public denunciations of both paganism and the ecclesiastical/political leaders for abuse of power. Saint John harmonized the liturgical prayers and rubrics of the Church, resulting in *The Divine Liturgy of Saint John Chrysostom* (Parry & Melling, 2001). Among his famous writings are hundreds of exegetical homilies on Scripture, and the treatises *On the Priesthood* and *On the Incomprehensibility of the Divine Nature*.

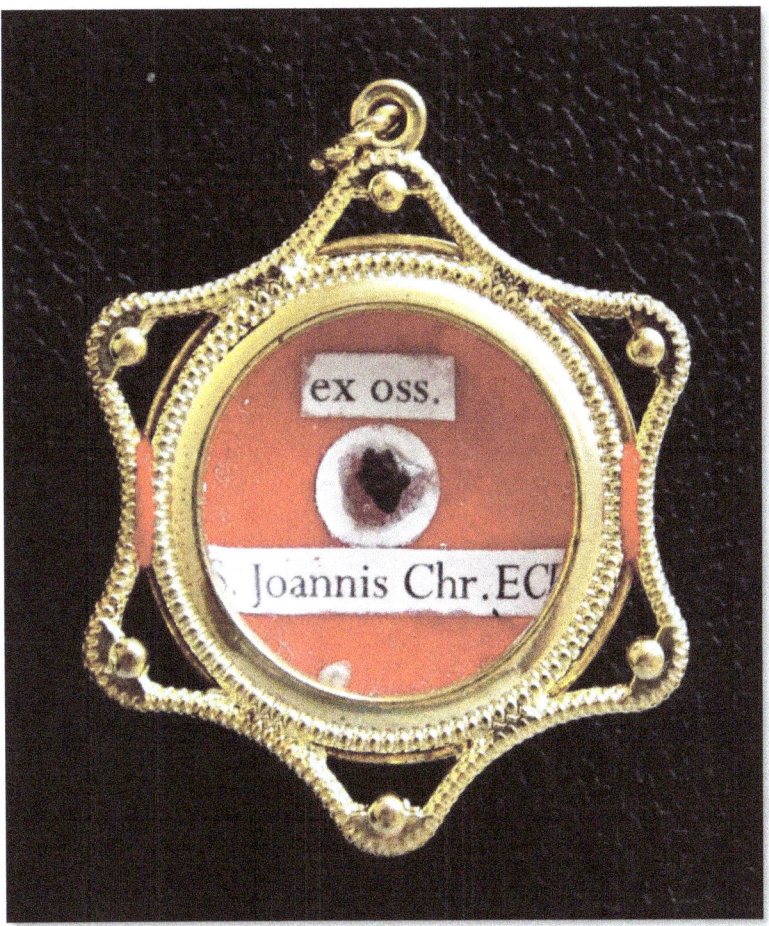

Ex ossibus Sancte Joannis

Small piece of bone of Saint John Chrysostom, Doctor and Bishop. His relics were translated from Comana, Armenia to the Imperial Polyandreion in Constantinople in 438. First class relic.

Saint John Nepomucene Neumann

Saint John Nepomucene Neumann (1811 – 1860) was a destitute Bohemian immigrant to the US. He became a priest with the Congregation of the Most Holy Redeemer, visiting the sick village to village, at times celebrating the holy liturgy on kitchen tables (The Redemptorists of the Baltimore Province, 2015). He became the fourth bishop of Philadelphia and the first naturalized American bishop to be canonized. Saint John founded the Catholic diocesan school system in the US, the American division of the School Sisters of Notre Dame, and the Third Order of Saint Francis of Glen Riddle.

Ex ossibus Saint John Neumann

Small piece of bone of Saint John Nepomucene Neumann, Bishop. His remains can be found in a glass encasement beneath the altar in the lower church at the National Shrine of Saint John Neumann, Philadelphia, Pennsylvania, USA. First class relic.

SAINT MARCELLA OF ROME

Saint Marcella (325 – 410) was a beautiful, fashionable matron from Rome, Italy who founded monasticism among noble women after the early death of her husband (Burns & Farmer, 1995). She refused the advances of the Roman Consul Cerealis and turned her palatial home into a refuge for the poor, whereby Saint Jerome spent three years translating the Holy Bible into Latin. He called her "the glory of Roman women." Saint Marcella died after being tortured by the Goths when, under Alaric, they pillaged Rome, after she refused to reveal that she had given away all her wealth to charity (Butler, 1894).

Ex ossibus Saint Marcella

Small piece of bone of Saint Marcella, Martyr. Her relics were kept by her followers and can now be found in various places throughout Europe, particularly in Italy. First class relic.

SAINT MAXIMUS THE HAGIORITE

Saint Maximus the Hagiorite (the Greek; c. 1475 – 1556) was originally from Epiros, Greece. He became a monk, scholar, publicist, and translator active in Russia (Orthodox Church in America, 1996). Saint Maximus translated into Slavonic the *Annotated Psalter* that became approved for use by the Russian clergy and the Great Prince, Basil III. He also corrected the books for the divine service. Saint Maximus was imprisoned for challenging the Grand Prince for wanting to divorce his wife, during which time the saint wrote a Canon to the Holy Spirit in charcoal on the walls of the prison where he was being held.

Ex ossibus Saint Maximus

Small piece of bone of Saint Maximus the Hagiorite. His remains can be found at the northwest wall of the Church of the Holy Spirit at Holy Trinity-Saint Sergius Lavra, Moscow, Russia. First class relic.

SAINT RAFAELA MARIA PORRAS

Saint Rafaela Maria Porras (1850 – 1925) was the daughter of the Mayor of Pedro Abad, Spain, who became an orphan by late adolescence (Burns & Farmer, 1995). She founded the Congregation of the Handmaids of the Sacred Heart of Jesus, dedicated to the education of children and the poor. Later, this congregation became an Institute that she headed as Superior General. Saint Rafaela was persecuted by both her biological sister when the latter became superior and the very community she had founded, being banished to doing housework in a faraway house in Rome, Italy for 32 years.

Ex carne Sancta Rafaela Maria Porras

Small piece of flesh of Saint Rafaela Maria Porras, Foundress. Her remains can be found underneath the altar at the Basilica del Sacro Cuore di Gesù, Rome, Italy. First class relic.

SAINT ROMUALD

Saint Romuald (c. 951 – c. 1027) was an Italian youth who retired to a monastery after having witnessed his aristocratic father kill a relative in a duel over property (Burns & Farmer, 1995). He became a monk, then abbot at the same monastery. Saint Romuald founded the Order of Camaldolese Hermits to give structure to the eremitic, cenobitic rule of life that was reminiscent of that led by the Desert Fathers. Saint Romuald reformed over 100 hermitages and monasteries.

Ex ossibus Sancte Romualdi

Small piece of bone of Saint Romuald, Abbot. His remains can be found enshrined in the crypt of the Chiesa dei Santi Biagio e Romoaldo, Fabriano, Macerata, Italy. First class relic.

SAINT SEBASTIAN

Saint Sebastian (c. 256 – 287) was a Roman soldier and captain of the Praetorian Guard under the Emperor Diocletian and the Emperor Maximian (Butler, 1894). He was tied to the stake and shot to death with arrows upon disclosing his Christian faith, which Diocletian interpreted as grave betrayal. But Saint Sebastian failed to die. He then publicly harangued Diocletian for his persecution of Christians, at which the Emperor ordered the saint beaten to death with cudgels and his body thrown into the common sewer.

Ex ossibus Saint Sebastian

Small piece of bone of Saint Sebastian, Military Martyr. His remains can be found enshrined at the church of San Sebastiano Fuori le Mura, Rome, Italy. First class relic.

SAINT SERAPHIM OF SAROV

Saint Seraphim of Sarov (the Wonderworker; c. 1754 – 1833) is one of the most renowned ascetics of the Eastern Church, and the greatest 19th century *staretz* and healer (Orthodox Church in America, 1996). Originally from Kursk, Russia, he reportedly had many visitations from Jesus Christ, the Theotokos, angels, and saints since childhood. He became a monk and lived as a hermit for 25 years, often becoming transfigured. Saint Seraphim taught that the purpose of the Christian life was to acquire the Holy Spirit. He extended the monastic teachings of contemplation, self-denial, and theoria to lay people.

Ex ossibus Saint Seraphim

Small pieces of bone of Saint Seraphim of Sarov, the Wonderworker. His body can be found near the altar in the Cathedral of the Dormition, Moscow, Russia. First class relic.

Saint Thomas Aquinas

Saint Thomas Aquinas (1225 – 1274) is a Doctor of the Church, father of the Thomistic school of theology, and one of the most influential thinkers of medieval Scholasticism (Stump, 2003). Originally from Aquino, Lazio, Italy, he became a priest with the Order of Preachers and significantly influenced the fields of ethics, law, metaphysics, philosophy, and political theory, by synthesizing the Aristotelian principles of reason with the theological principles of the Christian faith. Among the most famous writings of Saint Thomas are the *Summa Theologica* and the *Summa contra Gentiles*.

Ex ossibus Sancte Thomae

Small piece of bone of Saint Thomas Aquinas, Doctor. His relics can be found at the Convent des Jacobins, Toulouse, France; the Cattedrale di Aquino, Lazio, Italy; and the Chiesa di San Domenico Maggiore, Naples, Italy. First class relic.

THE THREE KINGS

The Three Kings (Three Wise Men; BC – AC) were the Magi Melchior, king of Persia; Caspar, king of India; and Balthazar, king of Arabia. They visited the Christ Child on His Nativity and gave Him the legendary gifts of gold, frankincense, and myrrh (*Encyclopedia Britannica;* Nersessian, 2001). The kings were questioned by King Herod about the whereabouts of the Child Jesus, whom Herod perceived to be a great threat to his earthly kingdom, but the kings returned to their home countries by a different route, not to divulge the location of Jesus Christ. The three kings were martyred for their faith.

Ex ossibus Sancti Regis Magorum

Small piece of bone of the Three Kings, the Holy Magi. Their remains were originally venerated in Constantinople after having been discovered by Saint Helen, then translated to Milan, Italy in 344. Their bones can now be found at the Shrine of the Three Kings in the Hohen Domkirsche zu Köln, Cologne, Germany. First class relic.

RELICS OF THE SAINTS

FEBRUARY

SAINT AGATHA

Saint Agatha (231 – 251) was a virgin from Catania, Sicily. Born to a rich, noble family, at about 15 years of age she publicly attacked the Roman cult of images as idols and rejected the advances of the Roman Prefect Quintius, who then persecuted her for the Christian faith (D'Arrigo, 1986). Saint Agatha was imprisoned and tortured, her breasts were excised, and she was condemned to be burned at the stake. But an earthquake saved the saint's life and she was returned to prison, where she reportedly received a visitation from the Apostle Peter who healed her wounds. Saint Agatha died in prison.

Ex ossibus Sancta Agathae

Small piece of bone of Saint Agatha, Virgin and Martyr. Her head and some of her limbs can be found at the Chiesa della Badia di Sant'Agata, Catania, Sicily. One of the saint's arms can be found at the Cappella Regia di San Pietro, Palermo, Sicily; whereas her other arm can be found in Messina, Sicily. First class relic.

BLESSED ANGELO OF FURCI

Blessed Angelo of Furci (1246 – 1327) was an Italian Catholic priest with the Order of the Hermits of Saint Augustine. Born to originally barren parents, Blessed Angelo was known for his holiness and gentleness, zeal for uprightness, and fervent charity (Rotelle, 2000). He was considered a brilliant teacher. Blessed Angelo was appointed as the first chair in Theology of the Order and prior of its Neapolitan province.

Ex ossibus Beato Angelo

Substantial piece of bone of Blessed Angelo of Furci. His body can be found at the Convento di Sant'Agostino alla Zecca, Naples, Italy. First class relic.

BLESSED ANSELM POLANCO FONTECHA

Blessed Anselm Polanco Fontecha (1881 – 1939) was a bishop with the Order of Saint Augustine. The son of modest farmers from Teruel, Spain, he showed great faith and humility, becoming provincial superior of the Order. He traveled to China, Colombia, Peru, the Philippines, and the US as a teacher and formator (Rotelle, 2000). Blessed Anselm was eventually appointed Bishop of Teruel. When the city fell to the Republican Army, he refused to rescind the Spanish Bishops' Letter which denounced the persecution of the Church. He was imprisoned, used as a human shield by soldiers, and assassinated in a gorge.

Ex ossibus Beatus Anselmi Polanco

Small piece of bone of Blessed Anselm Polanco Fontecha, Bishop and Martyr. His remains can be found at the Catedrale di Santa Maria de Teruel, Aragon, Spain. First class relic.

SAINT BLAISE

Saint Blaise (n. d. – c. 316) was a court physician, bishop of Sebastea in historical Armenia, and one of the 14 Holy Helpers. As bishop, he healed many physical ailments, including those of several animals who sought him out on their own for assistance (Kirsch, 1907). He then retired to a cave where he remained for years in prayer and contemplation. Saint Blaise was imprisoned for his Christian faith during the Diocletian persecution, repeatedly scourged with iron combs, and ultimately beheaded.

Ex ossibus Sancte Blasii

Bone fragments of Saint Blaise, Bishop and Martyr. Many of his remains can be found at the Basilica di San Biagio, Maratea, Potenza, Italy. The saint's head, a small bone from his throat, and his hands can be found at the Church of Saint Blaise, Dubrovnik, Croatia. First class relic.

SAINT CLAUDE DE LA COLOMBIÈRE

Saint Claude de la Colombière (1641 – 1682) was a missionary priest with the Society of Jesus, confessor, and ascetical writer (Loyola Press, 2015). The son of noble French parentage, he was known for his solid, serious sermons, and eventually became preacher to the Duchess of York who was later Queen of England. As superior of the Jesuits, he became the spiritual director of Sister Margaret Marie Alacoque and a zealous apostle of the devotion to the Sacred Heart. Saint Claude was imprisoned and exiled back to France for being part of an alleged plot by the Jesuits to kill Charles II.

Ex indumentis Sancte Claudii

Small piece of cloth of Saint Claude de la Colombière, Confessor. His relics can be found in the chapel of the Monastery of the Visitation, Paray-le-Monial, France. Second class relic.

SAINT CYRIL AND SAINT METHODIUS

Saints Cyril (827 – 869) and **Methodius** (815 – 884) were the Byzantine bishop brothers and confessors from Thessaloniki, Greece who earned the title "Equal to the Apostles [and] Apostles to the Slavs" for influencing the religio-cultural development of the Slavic people (*Encyclopedia Britannica;* Orthodox Church in America, 1996). They founded Slavonic literature by devising the Glagolithic (and its descendant Cyrillic) alphabet to translate Scripture into Church Slavonic, which became the liturgical language of the Eastern Church. They wrote the first Slavic Civil Code. Saints Cyril and Methodius are co-patrons of Europe.

Ex ossibus Saints Cyril and Methodius

Small pieces of bone of Saints Cyril and Methodius, Bishops and Confessors. Some remains of Saint Cyril are in the altar of his shrine-chapel at the Basilica di San Clemente, Rome, Italy. The body of Saint Methodius can be found at the Basilica of Saints Cyrillus and Methodius, Velehrad, Moravia, Czech Republic. First class relics.

SAINT CYRIL OF JERUSALEM

Saint Cyril of Jerusalem (c. 313 – 386) is a Doctor of the Church. He was a Patriarch of Jerusalem, distinguished theologian, and confessor (Walsh, 1991). Saint Cyril wrote about the appearance of a cross of light above Mount Calvary (Telfer, 1955). He also wrote with forceful simplicity about the healing power of forgiveness, the divinity of Jesus Christ, God, and the fragrance of the Holy Spirit. Saint Cyril was exiled many times by the Arian heretic Acacius for his teachings, and because the saint repeatedly sold imperial gifts and plate to buy food for the people when Jerusalem suffered food shortages (Young & Neal, 2010).

Ex ossibus Sancte Cyrilli

Small piece of bone of Saint Cyril of Jerusalem, Doctor, Bishop and Confessor. His remains were buried in a grave located on the Mount of Olives, Jerusalem, Israel. First class relic.

Saint Gabriel of the Addolorata and Saint Paul of the Cross

Saint Gabriel of the Addolorata (1838 – 1862) and **Saint Paul of the Cross** (1694 – 1775) were Italian members of the Congregation of the Passion of Jesus Christ. Saint Gabriel was a clerical student renowned for his cheerfulness and humility during illness, and had a great devotion to Our Lady of Sorrows (Lummer, 1920). Saint Paul was a convert, mystic, priest, and founder of the Congregation (Strambi, 1853). Saint Gabriel was considered a source of significant edification and inspiration to his fellow students with his humble attitude. Saint Paul was an indefatigable writer of more than 2000 letters of spiritual direction.

Ex ossibus Sancti Gabrielis et Pauli

Small pieces of bone of Saint Gabriel of the Addolorata and Saint Paul of the Cross. The remains of Saint Gabriel can be found at his shrine in the Basilica di San Gabriele dell'Addolorata, Isola del Gran Sasso d'Italia, Teramo, Italy. The remains of Saint Paul can be found at his shrine in the Basilica dei Santi Giovanni e Paulo al Celio, Rome, Italy. First class relics.

Ex corpore et cineribus Sancte Gabrielis

Small piece of the body and ashes of Saint Gabriel of the Addolorata.

Ex corpore Sancte Pauli

Small piece of the body of Saint Paul of the Cross.

THE JAPANESE MARTYRS

The Holy Japanese Martyrs (n. d. – 1597) were a group of 26 Christians, including converts and young boys, who were crucified in Nagasaki, Japan for their faith by order of the *daimyo* Hideyoshi Toyotomi. The martyrs were Saints Francis of Kyoto, Cosmas Takeya, Peter Sukejiro, Michael and Thomas Kozaki, James Kisai, Paul Miki, Paul and Louis Ibaraki, John of Goto, Anthony of Nagasaki, Pedro Bautista, Martin of the Ascension, Philip of Jesus, Gonzalo Garcia, Francisco Blanco, Francis of Saint Michael, Bonaventure and Matthias of Miyako, Leo Karasumaru, Joachim Sakakibara, Francis of Kyoto, Thomas Dangi, John Kinuya, Gabriel of Ise, and Paul Suzuki (Frois, 1587).

Ex cruce The Holy Japanese Martyrs

Thick sliver from a cross of the Holy Japanese Martyrs (bottom left). Second class relic.

SAINT JOSEPHINE BAKHITA

Saint Josephine Bakhita (c. 1869 – 1947) was a sister with the Canossian Daughters of Charity. The niece of a village chief in Darfur, Sudan, she was kidnapped as a child by Arab slave traders who sold her into slavery, whereby she was physically abused and permanently scarred by multiple owners; forced to walk barefoot over 600 miles, and convert to Islam (Hutchinson, 1999). Saint Josephine was bought by the Italian Vice Consul who treated her kindly and eventually left her with the Canossians. There she manifested great gentleness and a missionary spirit, with her mind on God and her heart in Africa (Dagnino, 1993).

Ex ossibus Sancta Josephinae Bakhita

Small piece of bone of Saint Josephine Bakhita. Her body is enshrined under the main altar of the Chiesa della Sacra Famiglia – Suore Canossiane, Schio, Veneto, Italy. First class relic.

Saint Miguel Febres Cordero Muñoz

Saint Miguel Febres Cordero Muñoz (1854 – 1910) was a member of the Institute of Brothers of the Christian Schools (2012). Born with crippling physical difficulties to a politically powerful family in Cuenca, Ecuador, he joined the Institute after heavy opposition and became an educator, writing various books on literature and linguistics. This earned him membership in the Academy of Letters of Ecuador, France, Spain, and Venezuela. Saint Miguel was known for his simplicity, imperturbable spirit, genuine concern for his students, and intense devotion to the Sacred Heart of Jesus and the Virgin Mary.

Ex ossibus Saint Miguel Febres Cordero

Small pieces of bone of Saint Michel Febres Cordero Muñoz. His incorruptible body was translated in 1937 to a sanctuary dedicated to him in Quito, Ecuador. First class relic.

SAINT PERPETUA AND SAINT FELICITY

Saints Perpetua and **Felicity** (d. 203) were catechumens who had been imprisoned, tortured, and executed for their Christian faith at the hands of a fierce cow and the sword of gladiators in the amphitheater at Carthage, Tunisia (Roberts, Donaldson, & Coxe, 1885). Saint Perpetua was a married noblewoman with a nursing infant, whereas Saint Felicity was her pregnant servant. The saints exhibited joy during their martyrdom, which was carried out to celebrate the birthday of the Emperor Publius Septimius Geta Augustus.

Ex ossibus Sancte Perpetuae et Felicitatis

Small pieces of bone of Saints Perpetua and Felicity, Martyrs. Their remains were buried in a tomb in Carthage, Tunisia, over which was built the Basilica Maiorum. Some relics of Saint Perpetua were eventually translated to the Paroisse Notre Dame, Vierzon, France. First class relics.

BLESSED PIUS IX

Blessed Pius IX (1792 – 1878) was the longest reigning elected Pope in the Catholic Church. He convened the First Vatican Council and proclaimed the dogma of the Immaculate Conception of the Blessed Virgin Mary (E*ncyclopedia Britannica;* John Paul II, 2000). He also declared Mary as Mediatrix of salvation in his encyclical *Ubi Primum,* and approved the request of the American bishops that the Immaculate Conception be invoked as Patroness of the US. Blessed Pius issued the *Syllabus of Errors,* condemning various heresies including modernism.

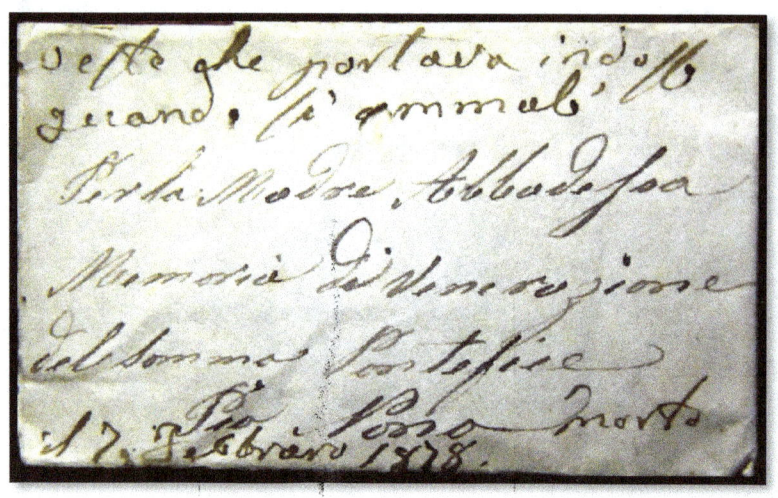

Ex veste Beatus Pius IX

Envelope containing a substantial rectangular piece from the linen vest that Blessed Pius IX was wearing when taken ill. On the envelope is written:

> *"Veste che portava indosso quando si ammalò. Per la Madre Abbadessa in memoria di venerazione del Sommo Pontefice Pio Nono, morto il 7 Febbraio 1878."*

> "Vest that he was wearing when he fell sick. For the Mother Abbess in venerable memory of the Holy Father Pius IX, who died on February 7, 1878."

The remains of Blessed Pius IX were enshrined in the Basilica di San Lorenzo Fuori le Mura, Rome, Italy until 2011, when they removed after severe flooding. Second class relic.

SAINT POLYCARP

Saint Polycarp (69 – 156) is one of the three Apostolic Fathers of the Church. He was one of the disciples of the Apostle John (Weidmann, 1999) who ordained him bishop of Smyrna, Turkey. He wrote the forceful *Epistle to the Philippians*, warning against apostasy (Brown, 1997), and corresponded with Saint Ignatius of Antioch. Saint Polycarp was burned at the stake, then stabbed with a spear after the fire had left him unharmed, for having refused to offer incense to the Emperor Marcus Aurelius (Wace, 2005).

Ex ossibus Sancte Policarpus

Small piece of bone of Saint Polycarp, Church Father, Bishop, and Martyr. His bones were gathered after his death. The saint's arm was translated in 1479 from Smyrna to the Monastery of the Panagia Ambelakiotissa – Saint Polycarp, Nafpaktos, Greece. First class relic.

SAINT SIMEON THE GOD-RECEIVER

Saint Simeon the God-Receiver (n. d.) was the righteous prophet of Jerusalem who held the Infant Christ in his arms during the Presentation of the Lord in the Temple (Lk 2:25-35). Saint Simeon was one of the group of 70 who had traveled to Alexandria to translate the Old Testament into the Greek *Septuagint*. Upon reaching the verse of Isaiah 7:14, he was about to correct the word *virgin* into *woman* as the former seemed inaccurate, when an angel appeared to him and said that he would not die before seeing Christ born of a pure, spotless Virgin (Orthodox Church in America, 1996).

Ex ossibus Saint Simeon

Small bone fragments of Saint Simeon the God-Receiver, Prophet. His relics were translated to a tomb in Constantinople in the 6th century. First class relic.

BLESSED SIMON FIDATI

Blessed Simon Fidati (c. 1295 – 1348) was an ascetic and confessor born to a distinguished family in Cascia, Italy. He joined the Order of the Hermits of Saint Augustine and became renowned as a brilliant, but humble, preacher and outstanding spiritual director (Rotelle, 2000). His most significant written work was *De Gestis Domini Salvatoris*. Blessed Simon founded a convent for women and a refuge for unmarried mothers.

Ex ossibus Beatus Simonis Fidati

Substantial piece of bone of Blessed Simon Fidati. His remains can be found in the crypt chapel at the Basilica di Santa Rita, Cascia, Italy. First class relic.

BLESSED STEFANO BELLESINI

Blessed Stefano Bellesini (1774 – 1840) was an Italian aristocrat who became a priest and novice master with the Order of the Hermits of Saint Augustine (Rotelle, 2000). He had great devotion to Our Lady of Good Counsel and was known for his interest in teaching children who were poor in the city of Trento, Italy, also giving them food and clothing. This resulted in Blessed Stefano being appointed superintendent of all the schools in his district by local authorities. But after he attempted to resume religious life in Rome, the authorities felt betrayed and Blessed Stefano was exiled, being forbidden to ever return.

Ex ossibus Blessed Stefano Bellesini

Large piece of bone of Blessed Stefano Bellesini. His relics can be found at the shrine of the Madonna del Buon Consiglio, Genazzano, Italy. First class relic.

SAINT VALENTINE

Saint Valentine (n. d. – 269) was bishop of Terni, Italy. He was repeatedly arrested for converting people to Christianity, marrying Christian couples, and aiding and abetting Christians persecuted by the Emperor Claudius Gothicus (Thurston, 1933). Saint Valentine was then sent to Rome and imprisoned, during which time he attempted to convert the Emperor. However, Claudius became enraged at such brazen defiance and sentenced Saint Valentine to be executed on the Via Flaminia, after the saint refused to denounce his faith.

Ex ossibus Sancte Valentini

Small piece of bone of Saint Valentine, Bishop and Martyr. His skull can be found at the Basilica di Santa Maria in Cosmedin, Rome, Italy; whereas some of his blood can be found at the Whitefriar Street Carmelite Church, Dublin, Ireland. More of the saint's relics can be found at the Birmingham Oratory, Birmingham, England; at the Stephansdom in Vienna, Austria; and at the Blessed John Duns Scotus Church, Glasgow, Scotland. First class relic.

REFERENCES

Brown, R. E. (1997). Early Christian Writings on Polycarp. In *An Introduction to the New Testament*. New Haven, CT: Yale University Press.

Burns, P., and Farmer, D. H. (Eds.). (1995). *Butler's Lives of the Saints: New Full Edition*. Collegeville, MN: Liturgical Press.

Butler, A. (1894). *Lives of the Saints*. New York: Benziger Brothers.

Congregation of the Holy Cross. (2014). *Saint André Bessette*. Retrieved in 2015.

Copt-Net Repository. (n. d.). *Saint Anthony: Father of the Monks*. Retrieved in 2015.

D'Arrigo, S. (1986). *Il Martirio di Sant'Agata Nel Quadro Storico del Suo Tempo*. Catania, Italy: Banca Monte di Pietà S. Agata.

Dagnino, M. L. (1993). *Bakhita Tells Her Story* (3rd ed.). Rome, Italy: Canossiane Figlie della Carità.

Encyclopedia Britannica. Magi. Retrieved in 2014.

Encyclopedia Britannica. Saints Cyril and Methodius. Retrieved in 2015.

Encyclopedia Britannica. Pius IX, Pope. Retrieved in 2015.

Emmitsburg Area Historical Society. (1996). *St. Elizabeth Ann Seton*. Retrieved in 2015.

First Council of Ephesus. (431). Retrieved in 2015.

Frois, L. (1597). Order of the Martyrs. In *Documents*. Nagasaki City, Japan: Twenty Six Martyrs Museum. Retrieved in 2015.

Herbermann, C. (Ed.). (1913). Ven. Angelo Paoli. In *Catholic Encyclopedia*. New York: Robert Appleton.

Holy Apostles Convent. (2001). *The Lives of the Three Great Hierarchs: Basil the Great, Gregory the Theologian, and John Chrysostom*. Buena Vista, CO: Holy Apostles Convent Publications.

Hutchinson, R. (1999). *Their Kingdom Come: Inside the Secret World of Opus Dei*. New York: St. Martin's Press.

Institute of the Brothers of the Christian Schools. (2012). *Saint Miguel Febres Cordero*. Retrieved in 2015.

John Paul II. (2000). Pope Pius IX – Homily of the Holy Father. In *L'Osservatore Romano*, September 6.

Kirsch, J. P. (1907). St. Blaise. In *Catholic Encyclopedia*. New York: Robert Appleton.

Loyola Press. St. Claude de la Colombière, SJ (1641–1682). In *Ignatian Spirituality*. Retrieved in 2015.

Lummer, R. (1920). *Saint Gabriel of Our Lady of Sorrows, Passionist: A Youthful Hero of Sanctity*. Whitefish, MT: Kessinger Publishing.

Matz, T. (2000). St. John Bosco. In *Catholic Online*, retrieved in 2015.

McGuckin, J. A. (2001). *Saint Gregory of Nazianzus: An Intellectual Biography.* Crestwood, NY: Saint Vladimir's Seminary Press.

McNamara, J. A., Halborg, J. E., and Whatley, E. G. (Eds. & Trans.). (1992). *Sainted Women of the Dark Ages.* Durham, NC: Duke University Press.

McSorley, J. (1907). St. Basil the Great. In *Catholic Encyclopedia.* New York: Robert Appleton.

Morrison, J. (1999). *The Educational Philosophy of Don Bosco.* Guwahati, India: Don Bosco Publications.

Nersessian, V. (2001). *The Bible in the Armenian Tradition.* Los Angeles, CA: Getty Publications

Orthodox Church in America. (1996). *Lives of the Saints.* Retrieved in 2015.

Parry, D., and Melling, D. (Eds.). (2001). St. John Chrysostom. In *The Blackwell Dictionary of Eastern Christianity.* Oxford, UK: Blackwell.

Pope Pius IX. (1854). *Ineffabilis Deus.* Retrieved in 2015.

Pope Pius XII. (1950). *Munificentissimus Deus.* Retrieved in 2015.

_____. (1954). *Ad Caeli Reginam.* Retrieved in 2015.

Roberts, A., Donaldson, J., and Coxe, A. C. (1885). The Passion of the Holy Martyrs Perpetua and Felicity. In *Ante-Nicene Fathers* (Vol. 3; Trans. R. E. Wallis). Buffalo, NY: Christian Literature Publishing.

Rotelle, J. (2000). *Book of Augustinian Saints.* Villanova, PA: Augustinian Press.

Schaff, P. (2009). *Nicene and Post-Nicene Fathers Series II, Volume 10* (Enhanced Version, Kindle ed.).

_____. (2012). *Nicene and Post-Nicene Fathers Series II, Volume IX* (Kindle ed.).

_____. (2013). *Nicene and Post-Nicene Fathers Series II, Volume 13* (Kindle ed.).

Second Council of Constantinople. (553). Retrieved in 2015.

Strambi, V. (1853). *The Life of Paul of the Cross.* London: Thomas Richardson.

Stump, E. (2003). *Aquinas.* London: Routledge.

Telfer, W. (1955). *Cyril of Jerusalem and Nemesius of Emesa.* Philadelphia: Westminster Press.

The British Province of Carmelites. (2013). *Saints of Carmel: Bl. Angelo Paoli – Friar.* Retrieved in 2015.

The Redemptorists of the Baltimore Province. (2015). *St. John Nepomucene Neumann.* Retrieved in 2015.

Thurston, H. (1933). St. Valentine, Martyr. In *Butler's Lives of the Saints* (Vol. II). New York: Benziger Brothers.

Wace, H. (2005). Polycarpus, Bishop of Smyrna. In *Dictionary of Christian Biography and Literature to the End of the Sixth Century A.D., with an Account of the Principal Sects and Heresies.* Grand Rapids, MI: Christian Classics Ethereal Library.

Walsh, M. (Ed.). (1991). *Butler's Lives of the Saints* (Rev., 1st Harper Collins ed.). San Francisco: Harper Collins.

Weidmann, F. W. (Ed.). (1999). *Polycarp and John: The Harris Fragments and Their Challenge to the Literary Tradition.* Notre Dame, IN: University of Notre Dame Press.

Young, F. M., and Neal, A. (2010). *From Nicaea to Chalcedon: A Guide to the Literature and its Background* (2nd ed.). Ada, MI: Baker Academic.

ABOUT THE AUTHORS

The Reverend Richard G. Cannuli, O.S.A., is professor of fine arts at Villanova University, Pennsylvania; a world-renowned iconographer, and liturgical consultant. Marcelle Bartolo-Abela is the author of several books on Christian spirituality in daily life.

Fr. Richard Cannuli

The Reverend Richard G. Cannuli, O.S.A., obtained the Bachelor of Fine Arts from Villanova University, Pennsylvania in 1973 and the Master of Fine Arts from the Platt Institute in Brooklyn, New York in 1978. He studied iconography under the Russian master-iconographer Vladislav Andrejev and watercolor in Siena, Italy. Cannuli joined the faculty at Villanova University, teaching courses on transparent watercolor, printmaking, oil painting, figure drawing, fabric and iconography. Cannuli is the founder and director of the art gallery of the university and curator of the university's art collection.

Cannuli was appointed full professor of fine arts in 2000. He chaired the Department of Studio Art, History of Art and Music at Villanova University for 11 years and the Department of Theatre, Studio Art and Music for five years. Besides being a noted iconographer, Cannuli is also a master watercolorist and world-renowned designer of liturgical vestments. In addition, he designs and works with stained glass windows, mosaic, fabric and liturgical furniture. Certified in liturgical design by the Chicago Theological Union, Cannuli has consulted for numerous religious communities on the construction of choir and chapel spaces in Italy and the US.

Cannuli has presented exhibits of his icons in Austria, Czech Republic, Italy, Japan, Lebanon, Poland, South Africa and the US. He has similarly presented watercolor exhibits in Belarus, China, Greece, Italy, Russia, Spain and the US. Cannuli has organized, curated and judged various art exhibitions and consulted on determining the symbolism of antique icons together with specialists from Belarus and Russia. Cannuli regularly conducts iconography workshops in the Czech Republic, England, Italy, Poland and the US.

Icons of Cannuli have been commissioned by several parish communities and private individuals both in Europe and the US. Some of these can be seen in his book *Approaching the Divine: A Primer for Iconography*, released by Hope and Life Press in 2014. Major commissions that Cannuli has written can be found at the chapel of the law school of Villanova University in Pennsylvania, the churches of Divine Mercy and Saint Francis Xavier in Philadelphia; the convent of Saint Augustine in San Gimigniano, Italy, and the monastery of the Holy Name of Jesus in Denmark, Wisconsin.

Cannuli's icon titled *Do Not Weep For Me, Mother* was presented on behalf of Villanova University to the Primate of the Maronite Church, His Eminence, Patriarch Nasrallah Peter Sfeir. His icon of *Saint Augustine* has been presented to His Holiness, Pope Francis on the occasion of the opening of the General Chapter of the Order of Saint Augustine. Cannuli's icon titled *The Holy Face Made Without Human Hands* was accepted into the permanent collection of the Holy Monastery of Saint Catherine at Mount Sinai, Egypt; a collection that portrays the best early icons worldwide.

HOPE AND LIFE PRESS BOOKS

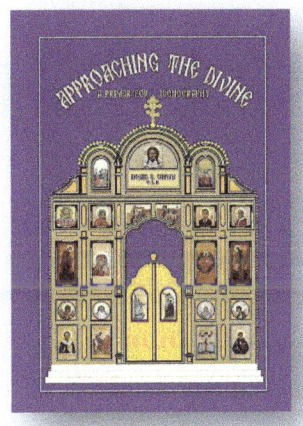

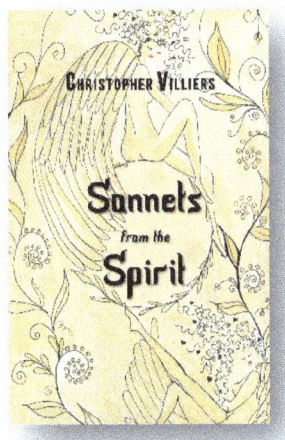

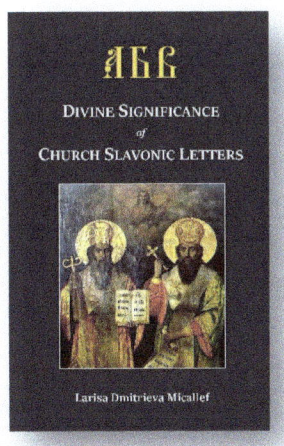
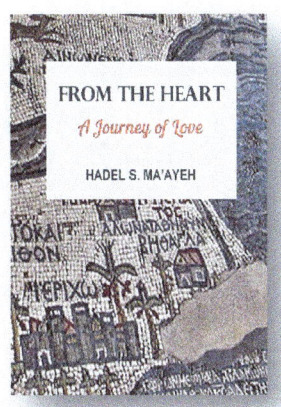

www.ingramcontent.com/pod-product-compliance
Lightning Source LLC
Chambersburg PA
CBHW082247300426
44110CB00039B/2462